THE GAMBLING ADDICTION
PATIENT WORKBOOK

THE GAMBLING ADDICTION PATIENT WORKBOOK

ROBERT R. PERKINSON
Keystone Treatment Center

SAGE Publications
International Educational and Professional Publisher
Thousand Oaks ■ London ■ New Delhi

For information:

Sage Publications, Inc.
2455 Teller Road
Thousand Oaks, California 91320
E-mail: order@sagepub.com

Sage Publications Ltd.
6 Bonhill Street
London EC2A 4PU
United Kingdom

Sage Publications India Pvt. Ltd.
B-42, Panchsheel Enclave
Post Box 4109
New Delhi 110 017 India

Printed in the United States of America

Library of Congress Cataloging-in-Publication Data

Perkinson, Robert R.
The gambling addiction patient workbook / by Robert R. Perkinson.
        p. cm.
Includes bibliographical references.
ISBN 0-7619-2867-7 (Paper)
    1. Compulsive gambling-Treatment-Problems, exercises, etc. I. Title.
RC569.5.G35P47 2003
616.85´8410651—dc211

                                                                2003000230

Printed on acid-free paper

             05   06   07   08   09   10   9   8   7   6   5   4   3

Acquiring Editor:	Margaret H. Seawell
Production Editor:	Claudia A. Hoffman
Copy Editor:	Jamie Robinson
Typesetter:	C&M Digitals (P) Ltd.
Cover Designer:	Michelle Lee

Contents

Introduction

Congratulations and welcome to treatment. You have made a monumental step in recovery from your addiction to gambling. You can be proud of yourself. You can feel confident that treatment works. Ninety-percent of patients who work this program stay free of their addiction. You will get your life back if you change a few simple things. These are called the tools of recovery. This program is not hard; it's easy, but you must do your part. It's going to take some work.

The illness of addiction is not you. You don't have feel bad about yourself. This illness is a disease that lives inside of you. You are not bad, the illness is bad. You will find that this illness has a life of its own and that it will fight for survival. It will do everything in its power to get you off track and get you back to addictive behaviors. The illness is cunning, baffling, and powerful. It often works out of your awareness, and to stay in recovery you must substitute healthy behaviors for unhealthy ones.

Addiction is a chronic relapsing brain disease. The brain has been hijacked by an illness. You must be disciplined and fight for your life. You are in a life and death struggle, and the war will be played out inside of your mind, body, and spirit. You are in for a fight for your life, but you are not alone. We are going to fight along with you.

There are three things that you can do that will bring the illness under control. These new behaviors may seem unnatural for you at first, but you must do them all. If you leave one of the tools out of your effort, your chances of recovery significantly decrease.

Let's briefly go over the tools so that you can begin to understand them. You have to do three things to stay free of the need to gamble: get honest, go to meetings, and get on a spiritual journey to a Higher Power of your own understanding.

HONESTY

You have to get honest because the disease must lie to operate. The illness lives in and grows in the self-told lie. Addiction cannot survive in the light of the truth. You must try from the beginning to be honest with yourself and others. You don't have to tell everyone everything, but you have to stop telling lies. Real problems with real people can't be solved until and unless the facts of the situation are known. Treatment is a never-ending search for the truth.

MEETINGS

You have to go to recovery group meetings and help others there. Nothing protects you against relapse like helping other addicts. This works when all else fails. You will find out that you are uniquely skilled at helping other addicts and that only you will do. You are the only one who will be there, at the right time, at the right place, to share a truth that moves another addict toward recovery. You might not feel like helping others right now. You might just want to help yourself, but that's not going to work. This is a program of the *we*, not a program of the *I*. At the core of addiction is self-centeredness. You are going to get out of self and get into helping others. This will restore your sense of purpose and make you feel good about yourself again. The illness says you are worthless, so you must prove it wrong. You can't be worthless and be helping others at the same time. These things are incompatible. By helping others, you will prove that the illness is wrong. So even if it's not like you, even if you feel like you don't fit in, even if you feel uncomfortable in groups, begin encouraging others in recovery. All you have to do is share your experience, strength, and hope.

HIGHER POWER

You have to get on a spiritual journey to a Higher Power of your own understanding. You don't have to be a religious person. This is a spiritual journey, not a religious one. All you have to do is be willing to seek a Higher Power of your own understanding. If you don't believe in God, that's fine, just be open-minded and willing. That's all you need to do to begin your recovery journey.

Now that's simple, isn't it? Get honest, go to meetings, and get on a spiritual journey to a Higher Power. You can do that. But remember, the illness is at work. The addict that lives inside of you is going to fight you every step of the way. That stinking thinking inside of your mind, body, and spirit is going to find reasons why you will not do each of these three things. It may say that if you tell people the whole truth about you, they won't like you. It may say that the meetings are boring and unnecessary. It may say that there is no Higher Power. The illness is going to fight for survival, and you must work hard to overcome it.

So that is the war. The battle lines are drawn. The enemy is confident of victory. You've tried to get free of your gambling addiction before, and you have always failed. The illness wants you to stay sick because it knows how important you are. It knows that if you get free, others will recover. Remember that you have an army on your side. You have a new family of brothers and sisters in recovery who understand you like no one else can. People working a good program of recovery know how to fight this illness, and they know how to win. Get ready, prepare yourself, and be willing to go to any lengths. Follow this program, and recovery is right up ahead. Soon you will restore your life and be happy, joyous, and free.

EXERCISES

The exercises that follow have been designed to take you step-by-step through the recovery program. Complete each exercise *only* when your counselor or sponsor says you are ready. Do not move ahead because you must practice and internalize the skills before you move on. Each exercise is a building block that leads to the next. If you move ahead too quickly you will not receive maximum benefit. If you were going to build a house, you wouldn't begin by putting up the roof. You have to begin with the foundation. Once the foundation is carefully laid down, you can begin with the walls, and finally the roof. So it is with recovery. Each step must be practiced and internalized before you move on to the next one. Your counselor or sponsor may give you exercises that are not in this book. These are for special problems that might make recovery more difficult for you. These exercises can be found in *Chemical Dependency Counseling: A Practical Guide* (Perkinson, 2002).

When you have completed an exercise, you will go over it in group or in a one-on-one session with your counselor or sponsor. When the group, counselor, or sponsor decides that you have successfully completed the exercise, you will move on to the next one. There is no right way or wrong way to do these exercises, just do the best you can and remember that honesty is the foundation of recovery.

Many people like to keep a journal of their recovery journey. I have thus provided blank pages for notes and journaling at the end of each section and at the back of the book, so that you can write down the parts of the program you want to remember in your journey from addiction to freedom.

Gambling History

This exercise will help you to become more aware of how gambling has affected your life and the lives of those around you. Answer the questions as completely as you can. It is time to get completely honest with yourself. Write down exactly what happened.

1. How old were you when you first gambled? Describe what happened and how you felt.

2. List all of the types of gambling you have ever participated in and the age at which you first gambled.

   Video lottery

   Black jack

   Bingo

   Scratch tickets

   Poker (cards)

   Horse racing

   Slot machines

   Powerball

   Sports betting

   Pull tabs

   Dog racing

   Other

3. What are your gambling habits? Where do you gamble? With whom? Under what circumstances?

4. Was there ever a period in your life when you gambled too much? Explain.

5. Has gambling ever caused a problem for you? Describe the problem or problems.

6. When you've gambled, have you found that you've gambled more, or for a longer period of time, than you had originally intended? Give some examples.

7. Do you have to gamble more now to get the same effect you got when you first started gambling? How much more?

8. Did you ever try to cut down on your gambling? Why did you try to cut down, and what happened to your attempt?

9. What did you do to cut down? Did you change the time, place, or game? Did you limit the amount ("I'll only spend $20 tonight")? Did you restrict your gambling to a certain time of day ("I'll only gamble after 5:00")?

10. Did you ever stop gambling completely? What happened? Why did you start again?

11. Did you spend a lot of time getting over your losses?

12. Were you ever so obsessed with gambling that you had a problem doing something that was potentially dangerous, such as driving a car? Give some examples.

13. Did you ever gamble so much that you missed work or school? Give some examples.

14. Did you ever miss family events or recreation because you were gambling? Give a few examples.

15. Did your gambling ever cause family problems? Give some examples.

16. Did you ever feel annoyed when someone talked to you about your gambling? Who was this person, and what did he or she say? Give some examples.

17. Did you ever feel bad or guilty about your gambling? Give some examples.

18. Did gambling ever cause you any psychological problems such as being depressed? Explain what happened.

19. Did gambling ever cause you any physical problems or make a physical problem worse? Give a few examples.

20. Did you ever lose track of time when you were gambling? Give some examples.

21. Did you ever get sick because you were gambling? Give some examples.

22. Did you ever have intense guilt because of gambling? Give some examples of how you felt.

23. Did you ever get nervous or suffer withdrawal symptoms when you quit gambling? Describe what happened to you when you stopped gambling.

24. Did you ever gamble to avoid symptoms of withdrawal? Give some examples of when you used gambling to control withdrawal symptoms.

25. Have you ever sought help for your gambling problem? When? Who did you see? Did the treatment help you? How?

26. Why do you continue to gamble? Give five reasons.

27. Why do you want to stop gambling? Give 10 reasons.

28. Has gambling ever affected your reputation? Describe what happened and how you felt.

29. Describe the feelings of guilt you have about your gambling. How do you feel about yourself?

30. How has gambling affected you financially? Give a few examples of how you have wasted money as a result of your addiction.

31. Has your ambition decreased due to your gambling? Give an example.

32. Has your addiction changed how you feel about yourself?

33. Are you as self-confident as you were before?

34. Describe the reasons why you want treatment now.

35. List all of the types of gambling you have been involved in during the past 6 months.

36. List how often you have gambled in the past 6 months and what amounts were involved.

37. List the life events that have been affected by your gambling (e.g., with regard to school, marriage, job, children).

38. Have you ever had legal problems because of your gambling? List each problem.

39. Have you ever lost a job because of your gambling? Describe what happened.

40. Do you want treatment for your gambling problem? List a few reasons why you want treatment.

Honesty

This is an exercise to help you get honest with yourself. In recovery it is essential to tell the truth. As you will hear at every Gamblers Anonymous meeting, this is a program of rigorous honesty. Those who do not recover are people who cannot, or will not, completely give themselves to this simple program.

Dishonesty to self and others distorts reality. You will never solve problems if you lie. You need to live in the facts. You must commit yourself to reality. This means accepting everything that is real.

People who are pathological gamblers think that they cannot tell the truth. If they do, they feel they will be rejected. The facts, however, are exactly the opposite. Unless you tell the truth, no one can accept you. People have to know you to accept you. If you keep secrets, you will never feel known or loved. We are only as sick as our secrets. If you keep secrets from people, you will never be close to them.

You can't be a practicing gambling addict without lying to yourself. You must lie, and believe the lies, or the illness cannot operate. All the lies are attempts to protect you from the truth. If you had known the truth, you would have known that you were sick, and needed treatment. This would have been frightening, so you kept the truth from yourself and from others. Let's face it, when you were gambling, you were not honest with yourself.

There are many ways you lied to yourself. This exercise will teach you exactly how you distorted reality, and it will start you toward a program of honesty. Answer each of the following as completely as you can.

1. *Denial:* Telling yourself or others, "I don't have a problem." Write down a few examples of when you used this technique to avoid dealing with the truth.

2. *Minimizing:* Making the problem smaller than it really was. You may have told yourself, or someone else, that your problem was not that bad. You may have told

someone you lost a little money when you lost a lot. Write down a few examples of when you distorted reality by making the problem seem smaller than it actually was.

3. *Hostility:* Becoming angry or making threats when someone confronted you about your gambling. Give a few examples.

4. *Rationalization:* Making an excuse, such as "I had a hard day," "Things are bad," "My relationship is bad," or "My financial situation is bad." Give a few examples of when you thought you had a good reason to gamble.

5. *Blaming:* Shifting the responsibility to someone else. Examples of blaming include "The police were out to get me" and "My wife is overreacting." Give an example of when you blamed someone else for a problem you caused by gambling.

6. *Intellectualizing:* Overanalyzing and thinking to excess about a problem avoids doing something about it. Examples of intellectualizing are "Sure I gamble some, but everyone I know gambles" and "I read this article, and it said that this is a gambling culture." Give an example of how you use intellectual data and statistics to justify your gambling.

7. *Diversion:* Bringing up another topic of conversation to avoid the issue. Give an example.

8. Make a list of five lies you told about your gambling to someone close to you.
   1.
   2.
   3.
   4.
   5.

9. Make a list of five lies about your gambling problem that you told to yourself.
   1.
   2.
   3.
   4.
   5.

10. Make a list of ten people to whom you have lied.
   1.
   2.
   3.
   4.
   5.
   6.

7.

8.

9.

10.

11. How do you feel about your lying? Describe how you feel about yourself when you lie.

12. What do you think will change in your life if you begin to tell the truth?

13. How do you use lies in other areas of your life?

14. When are you the most likely to lie? Is it when you've been gambling?

15. Why do you lie? What does it get you? Give five reasons.

16. Common forms of lying used by gamblers are listed below. Give a personal example of each. Be honest with yourself.
    a. Breaking promises:

    b. Pretending you haven't gambled when you have:

    c. Pretending that you remember how long you had been gambling when you actually lost all track of time:

d. Telling someone you gamble no more than others do:

e. Telling yourself you were in control of your gambling:

f. Telling someone you rarely gamble:

g. Hiding your gambling:

h. Hiding money for gambling:

i. Substituting gambling for other activities and telling others you just weren't interested in doing what they wanted to do:

j. Saying you were too sick too do something when you really wanted to gamble:

k. Pretending not to care about your gambling problem:

People who are pathological gamblers lie to avoid facing the truth. Lying makes them feel more comfortable, but in the long run, they end up feeling isolated and alone. Recovery demands living in the truth. It means being able to make statements such as those that follow: "I am a pathological gambler." "My life is unmanageable." "I am powerless over gambling." "I need help. I can't do this alone." All of these are honest statements from someone who is living in reality.

You can either get real and live in the real world, or you can live in a fantasy world of your own creation. In a fantasy world, you will never solve problems. If you get honest, it will enable you to begin to solve your problems. If you are real, you will be accepted for who and what you are.

Wake up tomorrow morning and promise yourself that you are going to be honest all day. Write down in a diary when you are tempted to lie. Watch your emotions when you lie. How does it feel? How do you feel about yourself? Write it all down. Keep a diary for five days and share it with your group. Tell the group how it feels to be honest.

Take a piece of paper and write the word *truth* on it, then tape it to your bathroom mirror. Commit yourself to rigorous honesty. You deserve to live a life filled with love and truth. You never need to lie again.

Step One

We admitted we were powerless over gambling—that our lives had become unmanageable.

—Gamblers Anonymous (1989b, p. 38)

Before beginning this exercise, read Step One in *G.A.: A New Beginning* (Gamblers Anonymous, 1989b).

No one likes to admit defeat. Our minds rebel at the very thought that we have lost control. We are big, strong, intelligent, and capable. How can it be that we are powerless? How can our lives be unmanageable? This exercise will help you to sort through your life and to make some important decisions. Answer as completely as you can each question that applies to you. This is an opportunity for you to get accurate. You need to search for the truth about yourself.

Let's pretend for a moment that you are the commander in a nuclear missile silo. You are in charge of a nuclear bomb. If you think about it, this is exactly the kind of control that you want over your life. You want to be in control of your thinking, feeling, and behavior. You want to be in control all of the time, not just some of the time. If you do something by accident, or if you do something foolishly, then you might hurt someone.

What is the first thing a compulsive gambler ought to do in order to stop gambling? The compulsive gambler needs to accept the fact that he or she is in the grip of a progressive illness and has a desire to get well. (Gamblers Anonymous, 1989a, p. 8)

To accept powerlessness and unmanageability, a gambler must look at the truth. People who are powerless over gambling do things that are harmful to themselves and others. They do most anything to stay in action—to keep gambling. Gamblers are *in action* when they plan a bet, make a bet, or wait for a bet to come in. Once the bet is in, they are out of action. Being in action is a primary goal of compulsive gamblers. By staying in action, gamblers feel how they want to feel. They escape reality. They live in a fantasy world of their own creation that leads to increasingly serious consequences. But gamblers do not consider the consequences of their behavior, and they will keep gambling until they are on the verge of death—unless they get honest with themselves.

POWERLESSNESS

People who are powerless do things that they feel bad or guilty about later. To gamble, they may lie, cheat, steal, hurt their family members, or do poor work. Make a list of the things that made you feel the most uncomfortable in the past.

People who are powerless will gradually lose respect for themselves. They will have difficulty in trusting themselves. In what ways have you lost respect for yourself due to gambling?

People who are powerless will do things that they do not remember doing. When gamblers gamble, they can lose all track of time. They might think that they have been gambling for only a few minutes when, in fact, they have been gambling for many hours. If you gamble enough, you cannot remember things properly. Describe several situations in which you lost track of time while you were gambling.

People who are powerless cannot keep promises they make to themselves or others. They promise that they will cut down on their gambling, and they don't. They promise that they will not gamble, and they do. They promise to be home, to be at work, to be at the Cub Scouts meeting, or to go to school, but they don't make it. They can't always do what they want to do. They disappoint themselves, and they lose trust in themselves. Other people lose trust in them. Gamblers can count on themselves some of the time, but they cannot count on themselves all of the time.

1. Have you made promises to yourself that you would cut down on your gambling? What happened to these promises?

2. Did you ever promise yourself that you would quit entirely? What happened to your promise?

3. Did you ever make a promise to someone that you did not keep because you were gambling? Give a few examples.

4. Are you reliable when you are gambling? Give a few examples of when you were not reliable.

People who are powerless lose control of their behavior. They do things that they would not normally do when not in action. They might get into fights. They might yell at people they love—their spouses, children, parents, or friends. They might say things that they don't mean. Have you ever gotten into a fight when you were gambling? Describe each instance.

The desire to gamble is very powerful. It makes a gambler feel irritable and impatient. People who are powerless say things that they don't mean. They say angry things that they feel bad about later. They might not remember everything they said, but the other person does remember. Have you ever said something that you did not mean? What did you say? What did you do?

People are powerless when they cannot deal with their feelings. They may gamble because they feel frightened, angry, or sad.

1. Have you ever gambled to cover up your feelings? Give some examples.

2. List the feelings that you have difficulty dealing with.

People are powerless when they are not safe. What convinces you that you no longer can gamble safely?

People are powerless when they know that they should do something, but they cannot make themselves do it. They might make a great effort to do the right thing, but they keep doing the wrong thing.

1. Could you cut down on your gambling every time you wanted for as long as you wanted?

2. Did gambling ever keep you from doing something at home that you thought you should do? Give some examples.

3. Did gambling ever keep you from going to work? Give some examples.

4. Did you ever lose a job because of your gambling? Write down what happened.

People are powerless when other people have to warn them that they are in trouble. You may have felt as though you were fine, but people close to you noticed that something was wrong. It probably was difficult for them to define just what was wrong, but they worried about you. It is difficult to confront people when they are wrong, so most people avoid the problem until they cannot stand the behavior anymore. When gamblers are confronted with their behavior, they feel annoyed and irritated. They want to be left alone with the lies that they are telling themselves. Has anyone ever talked to you about your gambling? Who was this? How did you feel?

People are powerless when they do not know the truth about themselves. Gamblers lie to themselves about how much they are gambling. They lie to themselves about how often they gamble. They lie to themselves about the amount of money they are losing, even when the losses are obvious. They blame others for their problems. Some common lies that they tell themselves include the following:

"I can quit anytime I want to."

"I only gamble a little."

"The police were out to get me."

"I only gamble when I want to."

"Everybody does it."

"I gamble, but I don't have a problem."

"Anybody can have financial problems."

"My friends won't like me if I don't gamble."

"I never have problems when I gamble."

"I can pay the money back later."

"From now on, I'll just gamble a little."

"When I win, I'm going to buy a present for my family."

Gamblers continue to lie to themselves to the very end. They hold on to their delusional thinking, and they believe that their lies are the truth. They deliberately lie to those close to them. They hide their gambling. They make their problems seem smaller than they actually are. They make excuses for why they are gambling. They refuse to see the truth.

1. Have you ever lied to yourself about your gambling? List some of the lies that you told yourself.

2. List the ways in which you tried to convince yourself that you did not have a gambling problem.

3. List some of the ways in which you tried to convince others that you did not have a gambling problem.

Therefore, it is not surprising that our gambling careers have been characterized by countless vain attempts to prove we could gamble like other people. The idea that somehow, some day, we will control our gambling is the great obsession of every compulsive gambler. The persistence of this illusion is astonishing. Many pursue it to the gates of prison, insanity, or death. (Gamblers Anonymous, 1989a, p. 2)

UNMANAGEABILITY

Imagine that you are the manager of a large corporation. You are responsible for how everything runs. If you are not a good manager, then the business will fail. You must carefully plan everything and carry out those plans well. You must be alert. You must know exactly where you are and where you are going. These are the skills that you need to manage your life effectively.

Gamblers are not good managers. They keep losing control. Their plans fall through. They cannot devise and stick to things long enough to see a solution. They are lying to themselves, so they do not know where they are. They feel confused. Their feelings are being manipulated by gambling, so they cannot use their feelings to give them energy and direction for problem solving.

You do not have to be a bad manager all of the time for your life to be out of control. It is worse to be a bad manager some of the time. It is totally confusing. Most people with addictions have flurries of productive activity during which they work too much. They work themselves to the bone, and then they let things slide. It is like being on a roller-coaster. Sometimes things are in control, and sometimes things are out of control. Things are up and down, and people with addictions never can predict which way things are going to be tomorrow.

People's lives are unmanageable when they have plans fall apart because they are gambling. Make a list of the plans that you failed to complete because of your gambling.

People's lives are unmanageable when they cannot manage their finances consistently.

1. List any money problems that you are having.

2. Is any of this trouble the result of your gambling? Explain how gambling has contributed to the problems.

People's lives are unmanageable when they cannot trust their own judgment.

1. Have you ever been so absorbed in your gambling that you did not know what was happening around you? Give a few examples.

2. Did you ever lie to yourself about your gambling? Explain how your lies contributed to your being unable to manage your life.

3. Have you ever made a decision while gambling that you were sorry about later? Give a few examples.

People's lives are unmanageable when they cannot work or play normally. Gamblers miss work and recreational activities because of their gambling. Have you ever missed work because you were gambling? List things you missed because of gambling.

Have you ever missed recreational or family activities because you were gambling? List the times.

People's lives are unmanageable when they are in trouble with other people or society. Gamblers break the rules of society to get their own way. They have problems with authority.

1. Have you ever been in legal trouble when you were gambling? Explain the legal problems you have had.

2. Have you ever had problems with your parents because of your gambling? Give examples.

3. Have you ever had problems in school because of your gambling? Give examples.

People's lives are unmanageable when they cannot consistently achieve goals. Gamblers reach out for what they want, but something keeps getting in the way. It does not seem fair. They keep falling short of their goals. Finally, they give up completely. They may have had the goals of going to school, getting a better job, working on family problems, getting in good physical condition, and/or going on a diet. No matter what the goals are, something keeps going wrong with the plans. Gamblers constantly try to blame someone else, but they cannot work long enough to reach their goals. Gamblers are good starters, but they are poor finishers. List the goals that you had for yourself that you did not achieve.

People's lives are unmanageable when they cannot use their feelings appropriately. Feelings give us energy and direction for problem solving. Gamblers manipulate their feelings by staying in action. Gambling gives them a different feeling. Gamblers become very confused about how they feel.

1. What feelings have you tried to alter with gambling?

2. How do you feel when you are gambling? Describe the feelings in detail.

People's lives are unmanageable when they violate their own rules by disregarding their morals and values. Gamblers compromise their values to continue gambling. They have the value not to lie, but they lie anyway. They have the value not to steal, but they steal anyway. They have the value to be loyal to spouses or friends, but when they are gambling they do not remain loyal. Their values and morals fall away, one by one. They end up doing things that they don't believe in. They know that they are doing the wrong things, but they do them anyway.

1. Did you ever lie to cover up your gambling? Give a few examples. How did you feel about yourself?

2. Were you ever disloyal when gambling? Give a few examples.

3. Did you ever steal or write bad checks to gamble? Explain what you did and how you felt about yourself later.

4. Did you ever break the law when gambling? Exactly what laws did you break, and how did you feel about yourself?

5. Did you ever hurt someone you loved while gambling? Give a few examples.

6. Did you treat yourself poorly by refusing to stop gambling when you knew that it was bad for you? Explain how you were feeling about yourself.

7. Did you stop going to religious services? How did this make feel about yourself?

People's lives are unmanageable when they continue to do something that gives them problems. Gambling creates severe financial problems. Even if gamblers are aware of the problems, they gamble anyway. They see gambling as the solution.

Gambling also causes psychological problems. Compulsive gambling makes people feel depressed, fearful, anxious, and/or angry. Even when gamblers are aware of these symptoms, they continue to gamble.

And gambling creates relationship problems. It causes family problems in the form of family fights as well as verbal and physical abuse. It causes interpersonal conflict at work, with family, and with friends. Gamblers withdraw and become isolated and alone.

1. Have you had any persistent physical problems caused by, or exacerbated by, your gambling? Describe the problems.

2. Have you had any persistent psychological problems, such as depression, that were caused by your gambling? Describe the problems.

3. Have you had persistent interpersonal conflicts that were exacerbated by your gambling? Describe the problems.

We know that no real compulsive gambler ever regains control. All of us felt at times we were regaining control, but such intervals—usually brief—were inevitably followed by still less control, which led in time to pitiful and incomprehensible demoralization. We are convinced that gamblers of our type are in the grip of a progressive illness. Over any considerable period of time, we get worse, never better. (Gamblers Anonymous, 1989a, p. 3)

You must have good reasons to work toward a new life that is free from gambling. Look over this exercise and list 10 reasons why you want to stop gambling.
1.
2.
3.
4.
5.
6.
7.
8.
9.
10.

After completing this exercise, take a long look at yourself. What is the truth?

1. Have there been times when you were powerless over gambling?

2. Have there been times when your life was unmanageable?

Step Two

> We came to believe that a power greater than ourselves could restore us to a normal way of thinking and living.
>
> — Gamblers Anonymous (1989b, p. 39)

Before beginning this exercise, read Step Two in *G.A.: A New Beginning* (Gamblers Anonymous, 1989b).

In Step One, you admitted that you were powerless over gambling and that your life was unmanageable. In Step Two, you need to see the insanity of your disease and seek a power greater than yourself. If you are powerless, then you need power. If your life is unmanageable, then you need a manager. Step Two will help you to decide who that manager can be.

Most gamblers revolt at the implications of the phrase "restore to a normal way of thinking and living." They think that they may have a gambling problem, but they do not feel as though they have been abnormal.

In Gamblers Anonymous (GA), the word *normal* means being of sound mind. Someone with a sound mind knows what is real and knows how to adapt to reality. A sound mind feels stable, safe, and secure. Someone who is abnormal cannot see reality and is unable to adapt. A person does not have to have all of reality distorted to be in trouble. If you miss some reality, then you ultimately will get lost. One wrong turn is all that it takes to end up in a ditch.

Going through life is like a long journey. You have a map given to you by your parents. The map shows the way in which to be happy. If you make some wrong turns along the way, then you will end up unhappy. This is what happens in gambling. Searching for happiness, you make wrong turns. You find out that our map is defective. Even if you followed your map perfectly, you still would be lost. What you need is a new map.

Gamblers Anonymous gives gamblers this new map. It puts up 12 signposts to show you the way. If you follow this map as millions of people have, then you will find the joy and happiness that you have been seeking. You have reached and passed the first signpost, Step One. You have decided that your life is powerless and unmanageable. Now you need a new power source. You need to find someone else who can manage your life.

Gamblers Anonymous is a spiritual program, and it directs you toward a spiritual solution. It is not a religious program. In GA, *spirituality* is defined as the relationship you have with yourself and all else. Religion is an organized system of faith and worship. Everyone has spirituality, but not everyone has religion.

You need to explore three relationships very carefully in Step Two: the relationships with yourself, with others, and with a Higher Power. This Higher Power can be any Higher Power of your choice. If you do not have a Higher Power right now, don't worry. Most of the members of Gamblers Anonymous started that way. Just be willing to consider that there is a power greater than you in the universe.

To explore these three relationships, you need to see the truth about yourself. If you see the truth, then you can find the way. First you must decide whether you were abnormal when you were gambling. Did you have a sound mind or not? Let's look at this issue carefully.

People are abnormal when they cannot remember what they did. They have memory problems. To be abnormal, they do not have to have memory problems all of the time; they just need to have them some of the time. People who gamble might not remember what happened to them when they were gambling. Long periods of time can pass during which gamblers are relatively unaware of their environment.

List any memory problems that you have had while gambling. Did you ever find that you had spent more time gambling that you remembered? Give a few examples.

People who are abnormal lose control over their behavior. They do things when they are gambling that they never would do otherwise. List three times when you lost control over your behavior while gambling.

1.
2.
3.

List three times when you could not control your gambling—when you told yourself to stop but you couldn't stop.

1.
2.
3.

People who are abnormal consider self-destruction. Did you ever consider hurting yourself when you were gambling or suffering from gambling losses? Describe what happened.

People who are abnormal feel emotionally unstable. Have you ever thought that you were going crazy because of your gambling? Describe this time in your life.

Have you recently felt emotionally unstable? Describe how you have been feeling.

People who are abnormal are so confused that they cannot get their lives in order. They frantically try to fix things, but problems remain out of control. List a few personal, family, work or school problems that you have not been able to control because of gambling.

People who are abnormal cannot see the truth about what is happening to them. People who are gambling hide their gambling from themselves and from others. They minimize their problems, rationalize them, and deny that there are problems. Do you feel that you have been completely honest with yourself? List some of the lies that you have been telling yourself.

People who are abnormal cut themselves off from healthy relationships. You might find that you cannot communicate with your spouse as well as you used to. You might not see your friends as often as you did. More and more of your life has become centered on gambling. List three relationships you have cut yourself off from because of gambling.

    1.

    2.

    3.

As your gambling increased, did you go to religious services less often?

List any relationships that you have damaged as a result of your gambling.

How has your relationship with God been affected by gambling?

People who are abnormal cannot deal with their feelings. Problem gamblers cannot deal with their feelings. They do not like how they feel, so they gamble to change their feelings. They may gamble to feel less afraid or sad. They may gamble to feel more powerful. List the feelings that you wanted to change by gambling.

Now look back over your responses. Get out your Step One exercise and read through it. Look at the truth about yourself. Look carefully at how you were thinking, feeling, and behaving. Make a decision. When you were gambling, do you think that you had a sound mind? If you were unsound at least some of the time, then you were abnormal. If you believe this to be true, then say this to yourself out loud: "I am powerless. My life is unmanageable. My mind is unsound. I have been abnormal in thinking and living. I have been insane."

A POWER GREATER THAN YOURSELF

Consider a power greater than yourself. What exists in the world that has greater power than you do—a river, a tornado, the universe, the sun? List five things that have greater power than you do.

1.
2.
3.
4.
5.

The first Higher Power that you need to consider is the power of the Gamblers Anonymous group. The group is more powerful than you are, just as ten hands are more powerful than two. Gamblers Anonymous operates in groups. The group works like a family. The group process is founded in love and trust. Each member shares his or her experience, strength, and hope in an attempt to help himself or herself and others. There is an atmosphere of anonymity. What you hear in group is confidential.

The group acts as a mirror reflecting you to yourself. The group members will help you to discover the truth about who you are. You have been deceiving yourself for a long time. The group will help you to uncover the lies. You will come to understand the old Gamblers Anonymous saying, "What we cannot do alone, we can do together." In group, you will have greater power over the disease because the group will see the whole truth better than you can.

You were not lying to hurt yourself; you were lying to protect yourself. In the process of building your lies, you cut yourself off from reality. This is how compulsive gambling works. You cannot recover from addiction by yourself. You need power coming from somewhere else. Begin by trusting your group. Keep an open mind.

You need to share in your group. The more you share, the closer you will get and the closer you get, the more you will share. If you take risks, then you will reap the rewards. You do not have to tell the group everything, but you need to share as much as you can. The group can help you to straighten out your thinking and restore you to sanity.

Many gamblers are afraid of a Higher Power. They fear that a Higher Power will punish them or treat them in the same way that their fathers or mothers did. They might fear losing control. List some of the fears that you have about a Higher Power.

Some gamblers have difficulty in trusting anyone. They have been so hurt by others that they do not want to take the chance of being hurt again. What has happened in your life that makes it difficult for you to trust?

What are some of the things you will need to see from a Higher Power that will show you that the Higher Power can be trusted?

Who is the most trustworthy person you have ever known? How has this person treated you?

What do you hope to gain by accepting a Higher Power?

Gamblers Anonymous wants you to come to believe in a power greater than yourself. You can accept any Higher Power that you feel can restore you to sanity. Your group, nature, your counselor, and your sponsor can all be helpful to you in this restoration. You must pick this Higher Power carefully. We suggest that you use Gamblers Anonymous as your Higher Power for now. It is a group of people who are recovering. They have found the way. This program ultimately will direct you toward a God of your own understanding.

Millions of gamblers have recovered because they were willing to reach out for God. Gamblers Anonymous makes it clear that nothing else will remove the obsession to gamble. Some people have so glorified their own lives that they believe that they are God. You are now at a major turning point. This is your opportunity: You can open your heart and let God in, or you can keep God out.

Remember that this is the beginning of a new life. To be new, you have to do things differently. All that the program is asking you to do is be open to the possibility that there is a power greater than yourself. Gamblers Anonymous does not demand that you believe in anything. The Twelve Steps are simply suggestions. You do not have to swallow all of this now, but you need to be open. Most recovering persons take Step Two a piece at a time.

First you need to learn how to trust yourself. You must learn how to consistently treat yourself well. What do you need to see from yourself that will show you that you are trustworthy?

Then you need to begin to trust your group. See whether the group members act consistently in your interest. They will not always tell you what you want to hear. No real friend would do that. They will give you the opportunity and encouragement to grow.

What will you need to see from the group members that will show you that they are trustworthy?

Every person has a unique spiritual journey. No one can start this journey with a closed mind. What is it going to take to show you that there is a God?

Step Two does not mean that we believe in God as God is presented in any religion. Remember that religion is an organized system of worship. It is human-made. Worship is a means of assigning worth to something. Many people have been so turned off by religion that the idea of God is unacceptable. "We found that some of the obstacles preventing us from attempting to believe were pride, ego, fear, self-centeredness, defiance, and grandiosity" (Gamblers Anonymous, 1989b, p. 40).

Describe the religious environment of your childhood. What was it like? What did you learn about God?

How did these early experiences influence the beliefs that you have today?

What experiences have caused you to doubt God?

Your willingness is essential to your recovery. Give some examples of your willingness to trust in a Higher Power of your choice. What are you willing to do?

Describe your current religious beliefs.

Explain the God of your own understanding.

List five reasons why a Higher Power will be good for you.

1.
2.
3.
4.
5.

If you asked the people in your GA group to describe God, you would get a variety of answers. Each person has his or her own understanding of God. It is this unique understanding that allows God to work individually for each person. God comes to each of us differently.

Through the ages, there have been two philosophical arguments against the existence of a God:

1. If there is a God, then where is God? Why does God not make himself more knowable?
2. If there is a God, and if God is all good, then why do bad things happen?

To understand these questions, you must understand what God is like and what God is doing. God created you to love. That is the only reason why you exist. God did not need you; God has no needs. God wants a loving relationship with you. God desires the most intimate friendship possible. That is why God lives inside of your thinking.

God knows that love necessitates freedom. God created you and gave you the freedom to make your own decisions. You can do things that God does not want you to do. If God placed his face in the sky or was so obvious that everyone worshipped him, then no one would have a free choice. This is why God exists in a gentle whisper inside your thoughts. You have to stop and listen to hear God. It is incredibly easy to keep God out, and it is incredibly easy to let God in. When you were abusing yourself, God was there encouraging you to love yourself. When you were lying to others and treating others poorly, God was there encouraging you to love others. God has loved you from the beginning.

It is difficult to deny God because God exists inside of you. To deny God is to deny an essential part of you. We all know instinctively what is right and what is wrong. We do not have to be taught these things. The rules are the same across every culture and group. No matter where or how you were raised, the moral laws are the same and everyone knows them. We know not to lie or steal. We know to help others. We know to love ourselves.

Bad things happen because God allows free will. People hurt each other when they make their own choices independent of God's will. They can break God's law, and when this happens there is great suffering. You probably have done some things you are ashamed of. You never would have felt this shame if you had followed God's plan.

"Where was God when I needed God?" many people cry. "Where was God when all those bad things were happening to me?" Well, the answer to those questions is that God was right there, loving you and encouraging you to see the truth. God never promises that life is not going to hurt. God promises that he is there, loving you all of the time.

Do not be discouraged if you doubt God. Your doubt about God is not bad; it is good. It means that you think and reason. You should not blindly accept things without proof. That would be foolish. What you must know is this: Only God can overcome your doubt. There is nothing you can do to make doubt go away. You can only trust that if you seek God, then God will find you. Once God finds you, your doubt will be removed. Only by swimming in the sea of doubt can you learn how to swim with strong strokes. This is how your faith gets strong. No one is asking you to accept God blindly. Follow your Gamblers Anonymous group. The group members know the way. Be willing to seek God. Open your heart and your mind in every way you know how. Seek the God of your understanding. Ask your clergyperson, counselor, or sponsor for some reading. Go at your own rate. Follow God in your own way. Soon you will find a peace that will surpass all of your understanding. This is the peace that people in the program call serenity.

Step Three

We made a decision to turn our will and our lives over to the care of this power of our own understanding.

— Gamblers Anonymous (1989b, p. 40)

Before beginning this exercise, read Step Three in *G.A.: A New Beginning* (Gamblers Anonymous, 1989b).

You have come a long way in the program, and you can feel proud of yourself. You have decided that you are powerless over gambling and that your life is unmanageable. You have decided that a Higher Power of some sort can restore you to normal thinking and living.

In Step Three, you will reach toward a Higher Power of your own understanding. This is the miracle that you have been searching for. It is the major focus of the Gamblers Anonymous program. This is a spiritual program that directs you toward ultimate truth. It is important that you be open to the possibility that there is a God. It is vital that you give this concept room to blossom and grow.

Many of us used our sponsor, other members, or the fellowship as this Higher Power, but eventually, as we proceeded with the work required in these steps, we came to believe this Higher Power to be a God of our own understanding. (Gamblers Anonymous, 1989b, p. 40)

Step Three should not confuse you. It calls for a decision to correct your character defects under spiritual supervision. You must make an honest effort to change your life.

The Gamblers Anonymous program is a spiritual one. Gamblers in recovery must have the honesty to look at their illness, the open-mindedness to apply the solution advocated in the program, and the willingness to apply this solution by proceeding on with the recovery process. If you are willing to seek God, then you will find God. That is GA's promise.

UNDERSTANDING THE MORAL LAW

All spirituality has, at its core, what is already inside of you. Your Higher Power lives inside of you. Inside of all of us, there is inherent goodness. In all cultures, and in all

---

lands, this goodness is expressed in what we call the moral law. Morality demands love in action and in truth. It is simply stated as follows: Love. This law is very powerful. If some stranger were drowning in a pool next to you, then this law would motivate you to help. Instinctively, you would feel driven to help, even if it put your own life at risk. The moral law is so important that it transcends our instinct for survival. You would try to save that drowning person at your own risk. This moral law is exactly the same everywhere—in every culture. It exists inside of everyone. It is written on our hearts. Even among thieves, love is valued.

When we survey religious thought, we come up with many different ideas about God and about how to worship God. But when we look at saints of the various religions, we see that they are living practically indistinguishable lives. They all are doing the same things. They do not lie, cheat, or steal. They believe in giving to others before they give to themselves. To believe in a Higher Power, you must believe that this good exists inside of you. You also must believe that there is more of this good outside of you. If you do not believe in a living, breathing God at this point, don't worry. Everyone in the program started where you are.

All people have a basic problem: We break the moral law, even if we believe in it. This fact means that something is wrong with us. We are incapable of following the moral law. Even though we would deem it unfair for someone to lie to us, occasionally we lie to someone else. We might see someone dressed in clothes that look terrible and, when asked, tell the person that he or she looks good. This is a lie. We would not want other people lying to us like that. In this and other situations, we do not obey the very moral law that we know is good. We might even stand by and watch another person drown.

You must ask yourself several questions. Where did we get this moral law? How did this law of behavior get started? Did it just evolve? The Gamblers Anonymous program believes that these good laws come from something good. People in the program believe that you can communicate with this goodness.

We do not know everything about the Higher Power. Much of God remains a mystery. If we look at science, we find the same thing; most of science is a mystery. We know very little about the primary elements of science such as gravity, the weak force, the strong force, and electromagnetic energy, but we make judgments about these elements using our experience. No one has ever seen an electron, but we are sure that it exists because we have some experience of it. It is the same with the Higher Power. We can know that there is a power greater than ourselves if we have some experience of this power. Both science and spirituality necessitate a faith based on experience.

Instinctively, people know that if they can get more goodness, they will have better lives. Spirituality must be practical. It must make your life better, or you will discard it. If you open yourself up to the spiritual part of the program, then you will feel better immediately.

By reading this exercise, you can begin to develop your relationship with a Higher Power. You will find true joy here if you try. Without some sort of a Higher Power, your recovery will be more difficult. A Higher Power can relieve you of your gambling problem as nothing else can. Many people achieve stable recovery without calling their Higher Power "God." That certainly is possible. There are many wonderful atheists and agnostics in the program. But the Gamblers Anonymous way is to reach for a God of your own understanding.

You can change things in your life. You really can. You do not have to drown in despair any longer. Be open-minded and willing. Trust a recovery program that has worked for millions.

THE KEY TO STEP THREE

The key to working Step Three is willingness. You must have the willingness to turn your life over to the care of God as you understand God. This is difficult for many people in the program because they think that they are still in control. They are completely fooled by this delusion. They feel that they know the right thing to do and that everything would be fine if others would just do things their way. This leads them to deep feelings of resentment and self-pity when people won't cooperate with their plan. No matter how hard they try to control everything, things keep getting out of control. Sometimes the harder they work, the worse things get.

HOW TO TURN YOUR LIFE OVER TO GOD

To arrest gambling, you have to stop playing God and let God take control. If you sincerely want this and you try, then it will be easy. Go to a quiet place and talk to God about your gambling. Say something like this: "God, I am lost. I can't do this anymore. I turn this situation over to you." Watch how you feel when you say this prayer. The next time you have a problem, stop and turn the problem over to your Higher Power. Say something like this: "God, I can't deal with this problem. You deal with it." See what happens.

Your Higher Power wants to show you the way. If you keep trying to find the way yourself, you will stay lost. You do not know the future; you do not know the path of the tornado.

Step Three offers no compromise. It calls for a decision. Exactly how you surrender and turn things over is not the point. The important thing is that you be willing to try. Can you see that it is necessary to give up your self-centeredness? Do you feel that it is time to turn things over to a power greater than yourself?

List the things you have to gain by turning your will and your life over to a Higher Power.

Why do you need to turn things over to a Higher Power?

People should not confuse organized religion with spirituality. In Step Two, you learned that spirituality deals with your relationships with yourself, with others, and with your Higher Power. Religion is an organized system of faith and worship. It is human-made, not God-made. It is humankind's way of interpreting God's plan. Religion can be very confusing, and it can drive people away from God. Are old religious ideas keeping you from God? If so, then how?

A great barrier to finding your Higher Power may be impatience. You may want to find God right now. You must understand that your spiritual growth is not set by you. You will grow spiritually when God feels that you are ready. Remember that we are turning this whole thing over. Each person has his or her unique spiritual journey. Each individual must have his or her own walk. Spiritual growth, not perfection, is your goal. All that you can do is seek the God of your understanding. When God knows that you are ready, God will find you.

Total surrender is necessary. If you are holding back, then you need to let go absolutely. Faith, willingness, and prayer will overcome all of the obstacles. Don't worry about your doubts; your doubts are normal. Just keep seeking.

List 10 ways in which you can seek God. Ask someone in the program, a clergyperson, or your counselor to help you.

1.
2.
3.
4.
5.
6.
7.
8.

   9.

  10.

What does the saying "Let go and let God" mean to you?

What are some ways in which you can put Step Three to work in your life?

What things in your life do you still want to control?

How can these things be handled better by turning them over to your Higher Power?

List five ways in which you allowed gambling to be the God in your life.

   1.

   2.

   3.

   4.

   5.

How did gambling separate you from God?

What changes have you noticed in yourself since you entered the program?

Of these changes, which of them occurred because you listened to someone other than yourself?

Make a list of the things that are holding you back from turning things over.

How do you see God caring for you?

How do you understand God now?

Write down your spiritual plan. What are you going to do on a daily basis to help your spiritual program grow?

HOW TO PRAY

Pray by reading the Step Three prayer once each day for a week. Say the words carefully out loud, and listen to yourself as you speak. Feel God beside you, and when you are ready, talk to God. Make prayer a dialogue, not a monologue. Talk to God and then listen for God's answer to come to you inside of your thinking.

God I offer myself to Thee—to build with me and to do with me as Thou wilt. Relieve me of the bondage of self, that I may better do Thy will. Take away my difficulties, that victory over them may bear witness to those I would help of Thy Power, Thy Love, and Thy Way of Life. May I do Thy will always! (Alcoholics Anonymous, 1976, p. 63)

Listen for God in others. God may speak to you through them. Look for God's actions in the group, in the weather, and in nature. Read scripture and seek God through your reading. Ask your counselor, sponsor, or clergyperson for some suggestions.

HOW TO MEDITATE

Take time to meditate each day. Sit in a quiet place for about 10 to 20 minutes and pay attention to your breathing. Ask God to come into your thinking and then empty your mind. Do not be nervous if there is only silence for a while. Listen for God's message for you. Write down any words or images that come into your mind. Keep a log of each meditation for a week.

Day 1.

Day 2.

Day 3.

Day 4.

Day 5.

Day 6.

Day 7.

Write down your spiritual plan. What are you going to do daily to help your spiritual program grow?

Trust that if you are seeking God, then God will find you—no matter who you are, no matter where you are. God loves you more than you can imagine. You are God's perfect child, created in God's image. God has great plans for you.

Step Four

We made a searching and fearless moral and financial inventory of ourselves.

— Gamblers Anonymous (1989b, p. 68)

Before beginning this exercise, read Step Four in *G.A.: A New Beginning* (Gamblers Anonymous, 1989b).

You are doing well in the program. You have admitted your powerlessness over gambling, and you have found a Higher Power that can restore you to normal thinking and living. Now you must take an inventory of yourself. You must know exactly what resources you have available, and you must examine the exact nature of your wrongs. You need to be detailed about the good things about you as well as the bad things about you. Only by taking this inventory will you know exactly where you are. Then you can decide where you are going.

In taking this inventory, you must be detailed and specific. It is the only way of seeing the complete impact of your disease. A part of the truth might be, "I told lies to my children." The complete truth might be, "To cover up my gambling losses, I told my children that I had cancer. They were terrified and cried for a long time." These two statements would be very different. Only the second statement tells the exact nature of the wrong and gives the person the opportunity to feel the full impact of the disclosure. You can see how important it is to put the whole truth before you at one time—the truth that will set you free.

The Fourth Step is a long autobiography. You should write it down carefully. Read this exercise before you start, and underline the things in it that pertain to you. You will want to come back and cover each of these issues in detail as you write. If the problem does not relate to you, then leave it blank. Examine exactly what you did wrong. Look for your mistakes, even where the situations were not totally your fault. Try to disregard what the other person did, and concentrate on yourself instead. In time, you will realize that the person who hurt you was spiritually sick. You need to ask God to help you forgive that person and to show that person the same understanding that you would want for yourself. You can pray that this person finds out the truth about himself or herself.

Review your natural desires carefully, and think about how you acted on them. You will see that some of them became the God of your life. Sex, food, money, relaxation, relationships, sleep, power, and influence all can become the major focus of our lives. The pursuit of these desires can take total control and can become the center of our existence.

Review your sexuality as you move through the inventory. Did you ever use someone else selfishly? Did you ever lie to get what you wanted? Did you coerce or force someone into doing something that he or she did not want to do? Who did you hurt, and exactly what did you do?

In working through the inventory, you will experience some pain. You will feel angry, sad, afraid, ashamed, embarrassed, guilty, and lonely. The Fourth Step is a grieving process. As you see your wrongs clearly, you may feel that no one will ever love you again. But remember that God created you in perfection. You are God's masterpiece. There is nothing wrong with you. You have just made some mistakes.

TAKING INVENTORY

A Basic Look at Right and Wrong

1. Take a look at your relationship with God. Has God come first in your life? Have you sought and followed God's will at all times?
   a. What were your idols—money, fame, position, alcohol, drugs, sex, power, relationships?
   b. Have you honored God with your language?
   c. Have you always set aside a day to improve your relationship with God?
   d. Have you loved, honored, and respected your parents?
   e. Do you have unresolved hate, anger, and resentments?
   f. Were you ever guilty of adulterous acts or thoughts?
   g. Have you ever cheated, misrepresented, made pressure deals, or had bad debts?
   h. Have you ever been guilty of slander or spreading gossip?
   i. Have you ever wanted something that belongs to someone else or felt envious or overly competitive?
2. Take a look at any false pride you may find in yourself. Egotistical vanity is too great an admiration of your self. Pride makes you your own law, your own moral judge, and your own God. Pride produces criticism, backstabbing, slander, and character assassinations that elevate your own ego. Pride makes you condemn as fools those who criticize you. Pride gives you excuses. It produces the following:
   a. Boasting or self-glorification
   b. Love of publicity
   c. Hypocrisy or pretending to be better than you are
   d. Hardheadedness or refusing to give up your will
   e. Discord or resenting anyone who crosses you
   f. Quarrelsomeness or quarreling whenever another person challenges your wishes
   g. Disobedience or refusing to submit your will to the will of superiors or to God
3. Take a look at any covetousness or avarice you find in yourself. These are perversions of humanity's God-given right to own things.

Do you desire wealth in the form of money or other things as an end in itself rather than as a means to an end such as taking care of the soul and body? In acquiring wealth in any form, do you disregard the rights of others? Are you dishonest? Do you give an honest day's work for an honest day's pay? How do you use what you have? Are you stingy with your family? Do you love money and possessions for these things in themselves? How excessive is your love of luxury? How do you preserve your wealth or increase it? Do you stoop to devices such as fraud and dishonesty in dealing with others? Do you try to fool yourself in these regards? Do you call stinginess "thrift"? Do you call questionable business "big business"? Do you call unreasonable hoarding "security"? If you currently have no money and little other wealth, then how and by what practice will you go about getting it later? Will you do almost anything to attain these things and kid yourself by giving your methods innocent names?

4. Take a look at any lust you may find in yourself. Lust is inordinate love and desires of the pleasures of the flesh.

Are you guilty of lust in any of its forms? Do you tell yourself that improper or undue indulgence in sexual activities is necessary? Do you treat people as objects of your desire rather than as God's perfect creations? Do you use pornography or think unhealthy sexual thoughts? Do you treat other people sexually in the same way you want to be treated?

5. Take a look at any envy you may find in yourself. Envy is sadness at another person's good fortune.

How envious are you? Do you dislike seeing others happy or successful, almost as though they have taken from you? Do you resent those who are smarter than you are? Do you ever criticize the good done by others because you secretly wish you had done it yourself for the honor or prestige to be gained? Are you ever envious enough to try to lower another person's reputation by starting, or engaging in, gossip about that person? Being envious includes calling religious people "hypocrites" because they go to religious services and try to be religiously good even though they are subject to human failings. Do you depreciate well-bred people by saying or feeling that they put on airs? Do you ever criticize educated, wise, or learned people because you envy their advantages? Do you genuinely love other people, or do you find them distasteful because you envy them?

6. Take a look at any anger you may find in yourself. Anger is a violent desire to punish others.

Do you ever fly into rages of temper, become revengeful, entertain urges to "get even," or express an "I won't let him get away with it" attitude? Do you ever resort to violence, clench your fists, or stomp about in a temper flare-up? Are you touchy, unduly sensitive, or impatient at the smallest slight? Do you murmur or grumble, even regarding small matters? Do you ignore the fact that anger prevents development of personality and halts spiritual progress? Do you realize at all times that anger disrupts mental poise and often ruins good judgment? Do you permit anger to rule you when you know that it blinds you to the rights of others? How can you excuse even small tantrums of temper when anger destroys the spirit of recollection that you need for compliance with the inspirations of God? Do you permit yourself to become angry when others are weak and become angry with you? Can you hope to entertain the serene spirit of God within your soul when you often are beset by angry flare-ups of even minor importance?

7. Take a look at any gluttony or overindulgence you may find in yourself. Gluttony is abuse of the pleasures God attached to the eating and drinking required for self-preservation.

Do you weaken your moral and intellectual life by excessive use of food and drink? Do you generally eat to excess and, thus, enslave your soul and character to the pleasures of the body beyond its reasonable needs? Do you kid yourself that you can be a "hog" without it affecting your moral life? When you've gambled, did you ever win big only to return and immediately gamble to win more? Did you gamble so much that your intellect and personality deteriorated; your memory, judgment, and concentration were affected; and your personal pride and social judgment vanished? Did you gamble so much that you developed a spirit of despair?

8. Take a look at any laziness you may find in yourself. Laziness is an illness of the will that causes you to neglect your duty.

Are you given to idleness, procrastination, nonchalance, and indifference to material things? Are you lukewarm in prayer? Do you hold self-discipline in contempt? Would you rather read a popular novel than study something requiring brain work such as the Gamblers Anonymous book (GA, 1989b)? Are you fainthearted in performing things that are morally or spiritually difficult? Are you ever listless, with aversion to effort in any form? Are you easily distracted from things spiritual, quickly turning to things temporal? Are you ever indolent to the extent that you perform work carelessly?

Personality Defects

1. *Selfishness:* Taking care of your own needs without regard for others
   a. The family would like an outing. You would like to gamble, golf, or fish. Who wins?
   b. Your child needs a new pair of shoes. You put off buying them until payday then gamble away the paycheck.
2. *Using alibis:* The highly developed art of justifying gambling and other undesirable behaviors through mental gymnastics
   a. "A few dollars won't hurt anything."
   b. "Starting tomorrow, I'm going to change."
   c. "If I didn't have a wife and family. . . ."
   d. "If I could start all over again. . . ."
   e. "A little gambling will help me to relax."
   f. "Nobody cares anyway."
   g. "I had a hard day."

3. *Dishonest thinking:* Taking truths or facts and twisting them to come up with the conclusions you need, such as in the following examples:
   a. "My girlfriend is going to raise the roof if I drop her. It is not fair to burden my wife with that sort of grief. Therefore, I will hang on to my girlfriend. This mess isn't her fault."
   b. "If I tell my family about the $500 bonus, then it will all go for bills, clothes, the dentist, and so on. I've got to have some gambling money. Why start a family argument?"
   c. "My husband dresses well and eats well. The kids are getting a good education. What more do they want from me?"

4. *Shame:* Feeling that something irreparable is wrong with you
   a. No matter how many people tell you it is okay, you continue to berate yourself.
   b. You keep going over and over your mistakes, wallowing in what a terrible person you are.

5. *Resentment:* Displeasure aroused by a real or imagined wrong or injury accompanied by irritation, exasperation, and/or hate
   a. You are fired from your job. Therefore, you hate the boss.
   b. Your sister warns you about excessive gambling. You get fighting mad at her.
   c. A co-worker is doing a good job and gets accolades. You hate his guts.
   d. You may have resentment toward a person or a group of people, or you may resent institutions, religions, and so on. Anger and resentment lead to bickering, friction, hatred, and unjust revenge. They bring out the worst of our immaturity and produce misery for us and all concerned.

6. *Intolerance:* Refusing to put up with beliefs, practices, customs, or habits that differ from your own
   a. Do you hate other people because they are of another race, come from a different country, or have a different religion? What would you do if you were one of those other persons? Would you kill yourself?
   b. Did you have any choice in being born a particular color or nationality?

7. *Impatience:* Unwillingness to calmly bear delay, opposition, pain, or bother
   A pathological gambler is someone who jumps on a horse and gallops off madly in all directions at the same time.
   a. Do you blow your stack when someone keeps you waiting?
   b. Did anyone ever have to wait for you?

8. *Phoniness:* Insincere behavior; a manifestation of false pride or the old false front
   a. You present your love with a present as evidence of your love. Just by pure coincidence, it helps to smooth over your last gambling binge.
   b. You buy new clothes because your business position demands it. Meanwhile, your family also could use food and clothes.

9. *Procrastination:* Putting off or postponing things that need to be done; the familiar "I'll do it tomorrow"
   a. Did little jobs, when put off, become big and almost impossible later? Did problems piling up contribute to gambling?

   b. Do you pamper yourself by doing things "my way," or do you attempt to put order and discipline into your life?

   c. Can you handle little jobs that you are asked to take care of, or do you feel picked on when asked to do them? Or, are you just too lazy or proud to do the little jobs?

10. *Self-pity:* Feeling sorry for yourself

   a. "People at the casinos are having fun with their gambling. Why can't I be like that?" This is the "woe is me" syndrome.

   b. "If I had that guy's money, I wouldn't have any problems." When you feel this way, visit an alcoholic ward, cancer ward, or children's hospital and then count your blessings.

11. *Easily hurt feelings*: Being overly sensitive to the slightest criticism

   a. "If I walk down the street and say 'Hello' to someone and the person doesn't answer, I'm hurt and mad."

   b. "I'm expecting my turn at the meeting, but the time runs out. I feel like that's a dirty trick."

   c. "I feel as though they are talking about me when they're really not."

12. *Fear:* Feeling an inner foreboding, whether real or imagined, of doom ahead
You suspect that our use of gambling, behavior, negligence, and so on are catching up with you. You fear the worst.

   a. When you learn to accept your powerlessness, ask God for help, and face yourself with honesty, the nightmare will be over.

13. *Depression:* Feeling sad or down most of the day

   a. You keep going over all of the things that are going wrong.

   b. You tend to think that the worst is going to happen.

14. *Feelings of inadequacy:* Feeling as though you cannot do whatever it is you are trying to do

   a. You hold on to a negative self-image, even when you succeed.

   b. Your feelings of failure will not go away.

15. *Perfectionism:* Feeling that you have to do everything perfectly all the time

   a. Even when you have done a good job, you find something wrong with it.

   b. When someone compliments you on something, you feel terrible because it could have been better.

   c. You let your expectations get too high.

Physical Liabilities

1. Diseases, disabilities, and other physical limitations about how you look or how your body functions
2. Sexual problems or hang-ups
3. Negative feelings about your appearance
4. Negative feelings about your age
5. Negative feelings about your gender

Time Out

If you have gone through the exercise to this point without coming up for air—it figures. Easy does it! Take this in reasonable stages. Assimilate each portion of the exercise thoughtfully. Reading this is important, but applying it is even more important. Take some time to think and rest, and let this settle in. Develop some sort of a workable daily plan. Include plenty of rest.

When compulsive gamblers stop gambling, a part of their lives is taken away from them. This is a terrible loss to sustain unless it is replaced by something else. We cannot just boot gambling out the window. It meant too much to us. It was how we faced life, the key to escape, and the tool for solving life's problems. In approaching a new way of life, a new set of tools is substituted. These are the Twelve Steps and the Gamblers Anonymous way of life.

The same principle applies when we eliminate our character defects. We replace them by substituting for them assets that are better adapted to a healthy lifestyle. As with substance use, you do not fight a defect; you replace it with something that works better. Use what follows for further character analysis and as a guide for character building. These are the new tools. The objective is not perfection; it is progress. You will be happy with the type of living that produces self-respect, respect and love for others, and security from the nightmare of gambling.

The Way to Recovery: Your Virtues

1. *Faith:* The act of leaving the part of your life that you cannot control (i.e., the future) to the care of a power greater than yourself, with the assurance that it will work out for your well-being
   This will be shaky at first, but with it comes a deep conviction.
   a. Faith is acquired through application—acceptance, daily prayer, and meditation.
   b. You depend on faith. You have faith that the lights will come on when you flip the switch, the car will start, and your co-workers will handle their end of things. If you had no faith, then you would come apart at the seams.
   c. Spiritual faith is the acceptance of your gifts, limitations, problems, and trials with equal gratitude, knowing that God has a plan for you. With "Thy will be done" as your daily guide, you will lose your fear and find yourself.
2. *Hope:* The feeling that what you desire also is possible
   Faith suggests reliance. You come to believe that a power greater than yourself will restore you to sanity. You hope to stay free of gambling, regain your self-respect, and love your family. Hope resolves itself into a driving force. It gives purpose to your daily living.
   a. Faith gives you direction, hope, and stamina to take action.
   b. Hope reflects a positive attitude. Things are going to work out for you if you work the program.
3. *Love:* The active involvement in someone's individual growth
   a. Love must occur in action and in truth.

b. In its deeper sense, love is the art of living realistically and fully, guided by spiritual awareness of your responsibilities and your debt of gratitude to God and to others.

Analysis: Have you used the qualities of faith, hope, and love in your past? How will they apply to your new way of life?

You Stay on Track Through Action: More Virtues

1. *Courtesy:* Some people are actually afraid to be gentle persons. They would rather be boors or self-pampering. It is in your interest to be courteous.
2. *Cheerfulness:* Circumstances do not determine your frame of mind—you do. "Today I will be cheerful. I will look for the beauty in life."
3. *Order:* Live today only. Organize one day at a time.
4. *Loyalty:* Be faithful to what you believe in.
5. *Use of time:* "I will use my time wisely."
6. *Punctuality:* This involves self-discipline, order, and consideration for others.
7. *Sincerity:* This is the mark of self-respect and genuineness. Sincerity carries conviction and generates enthusiasm. It is contagious.
8. *Caution in speech:* Watch your tongue. We are all capable of being vicious and thoughtless. Too often, the damage is irreparable.
9. *Kindness:* This is one of life's great satisfactions. You will not have real happiness until you have given of yourself. Practice this daily.
10. *Patience:* This is the antidote to resentments, self-pity, and impulsiveness.
11. *Tolerance:* This requires common courtesy, courage, and a "live and let live" attitude.
12. *Integrity:* This involves the ultimate qualifications of a human—honesty, loyalty, sincerity.
13. *Balance:* Do not take yourself too seriously. You get a better perspective when you can laugh at yourself.
14. *Gratitude:* The person without gratitude is filled with false pride. Gratitude is the honest recognition of help received. Use it often.

Analysis: In considering these virtues, ask where you failed and how that contributed to your accumulated problem. Ask what virtues you should pay attention to in this rebuilding program.

Physical Assets

1. *Physical health:* How healthy am I despite any ailments?

2. *Talents:* What am I good at?

3. *Age:* At my age, what can I offer to others?

4. *Sexuality:* How can I use my sexuality to express my love?

5. *Knowledge:* How can I use my knowledge and experience to help myself and others?

Mental Assets

1. Despite your problems, how healthy are you emotionally?
2. Do you care for others?
3. Are you kind?
4. Can you be patient?
5. Are you basically a good person?
6. Do you try to tell the truth?
7. Do you try to be forgiving?
8. Can you be enthusiastic?
9. Are you sensitive to the needs of others?
10. Can you be serene?
11. Are you going to try to be sincere?
12. Are you going to try to bring order and self-control into your life?
13. Are you going to accept the responsibility for your own behavior and stop blaming others for everything?
14. How are you going to use your intelligence?
15. Are you going to seek God?
16. How might you improve your mind furthering your education?
17. Are you going to be grateful for what you have?
18. How can you improve your honesty, reliability, and integrity?
19. In what areas of your life do you find joy and happiness?
20. Are you humble and working on eliminating your false pride?
21. Are you seeking the God of your own understanding?
22. In what ways can you better accept your own limitations and the limitations of others?
23. Are you willing to trust and follow the Higher Power of your own understanding?

WRITING YOUR AUTOBIOGRAPHY

Using this exercise, write your autobiography. Cover your life in 5-year intervals. Be brief, but try not to miss anything. Tell the whole truth. Write down exactly what you did. Consider all of the things you marked during the exercise. Read the exercise again if you need to do so. Make an exhaustive and honest consideration of your past and present. Make a complete financial inventory. Mark down all debts. Exactly who do you owe, and what amount do you owe? Do not leave out relatives or friends. List every person and every institution that you have harmed with your gambling, and detail exactly how you were unfair. Cover both assets and liabilities carefully. You will rebuild your life on the solid building blocks of your assets. These are the tools of recovery. Omit nothing because of shame, embarrassment, or fear. Determine the thoughts, feelings, and actions that plagued you. You want to meet these problems face to face and see them in writing. If you wish, you may destroy your inventory after completing the Fifth Step. Many people hold a ceremony in which they burn their Fourth Step inventories. This symbolizes that they are leaving the old life behind. They are starting a new life free of the past.

Step Five

We admitted to ourselves and to another human being the exact nature of our wrongs.

—Gamblers Anonymous (1989b, p. 69)

Before beginning this exercise, read Step Five in *G.A.: A New Beginning* (Gamblers Anonymous, 1989b).

With Steps One to Four behind you, it is now time to clean house and start over. You must free yourself of all the guilt and shame and go forward in faith. The Fifth Step is meant to right the wrongs with others and your Higher Power. You will develop new attitudes and a new relationship with yourself, others, and the Higher Power of your own understanding. You have admitted your powerlessness, and you have identified your liabilities and assets in the personal inventory. Now it is time to get right with yourself.

You will do this by admitting to yourself, and to another person, the exact nature of your wrongs. In your Fifth Step, you are going to cover all of your assets and liabilities detailed in the Fourth Step. You are going to tell one person the whole truth at one time. This person is important because he or she is a symbol of God and all humankind. You must watch this person's face. The illness has been telling you that if you tell anyone the whole truth about you, then that person will not like you. That is a lie, and you are going to prove that it is a lie. The truth is this: Unless you tell people the whole truth, they cannot like you. You must actually see yourself tell someone the whole truth at one time and watch that individual's reaction.

It is very difficult to discuss your faults with someone. It is hard enough just thinking about them yourself. But this is a necessary step. It will help to free you from the disease. You must tell this person everything, the whole story, all of the things that you are afraid to share. If you withhold anything, then you will not get the relief you need to start over. You will be carrying around excess baggage. You do not need to do this to yourself. Time after time, newcomers have tried to keep to themselves certain facts about their lives. Trying to avoid this humbling experience, they have turned to easier methods. Almost invariably, they wound up gambling again. Having persevered with the rest of the program, they wondered why they failed. The reason is that they never completed their housecleaning. They took inventory all right, but they hung on to some of the worst items in stock. They only *thought* that they had lost their egotism. They only *thought* that they had humbled themselves. But they had not learned enough of humility and honesty in the sense necessary because they had not told someone their whole life stories.

By finally telling someone the whole truth, you will rid yourself of that terrible sense of isolation and loneliness. You will feel a new sense of belonging, acceptance, and freedom. If you do not feel relief immediately, don't worry. If you have been completely honest, then the relief will come. The dammed-up emotions of years will break out of their confinement and, miraculously, will vanish as soon as they are exposed.

The Fifth Step will develop within you a new humbleness of character that is necessary for normal living. You will come to recognize clearly who and what you are. When you are honest with another person, it confirms that you can be honest with yourself, others, and your Higher Power.

The person you will share your Fifth Step with should be chosen carefully. Many people find a clergyperson, who is experienced in hearing Fifth Steps, to be a good option. Someone further along in the Gamblers Anonymous program might also be a good choice. It is recommended that you meet with this person several times before you do the step. You need to decide whether you can trust this person. Do you feel that this person will keep your confidence? Do you feel comfortable with this person? Do you feel safe with this person? Do you feel that this person will understand you?

Once you have chosen the person, put your false pride aside and go for it. Tell the individual everything about yourself. Do not leave one stone unturned. Tell about all of the good things, and about all of the bad things, that you have done. Share the details, and do not leave anything out. If it troubles you even a little, then share it. Let it all hang out to be examined by that other person. Every good and bad part needs to be revealed. After you are done, you will be free of the slavery to lies. The truth will set you free.

Relapse Prevention

There is some bad news about relapse, and there is some good news. The bad news is that many patients have problems with relapse in early recovery. About two thirds of patients coming out of addiction programs relapse within 3 months of leaving treatment (Hunt, Barnett, & Branch, 1971). The good news is that most people who go through treatment ultimately achieve a stable recovery (Frances, Bucky, & Alexopolos, 1984). Relapse does not have to happen to you, and even if it does, you can do something about it. Relapse prevention is a daily program that can prevent relapse. It also can stop a lapse from becoming a disaster. This relapse prevention exercise has been developed using a combination of the models of Gorski and Miller (1986) and Marlatt and Gordon (1985). This exercise also uses both the disease concept model and a cognitive behavioral approach.

RELAPSE IS A PROCESS

Relapse begins long before you gamble again. There are symptoms that precede gambling. This relapse prevention exercise teaches how to identify and control these symptoms before they lead to problems. If you allow these symptoms to go on without acting on them, then gambling will result.

The Relapse Warning Signs

All relapse begins with warning signs that will signal you or your loved ones that you are in trouble. If you do not recognize these signs, then you will decompensate and finally return to gambling again. All of the signs are reactions to stress, and they are a reemergence of the disease. They are a means by which your body and mind are telling you that you are having problems. Gorski and Miller (1982) recognized 37 warning signs in alcoholics who relapsed. You might not have all of these symptoms before you begin gambling again, but you will have some of them long before you gamble.

You must determine which symptoms are the most characteristic of you, and you must come up with coping skills for dealing with each symptom. Listed next are the 37 warning symptoms. Circle the ones that you have experienced before you gambled.

1. Apprehension about well-being
2. Denial
3. Adamant commitment to stop gambling

4. Compulsive attempts to impose abstinence on others
5. Defensiveness
6. Compulsive behavior
7. Impulsive behavior
8. Loneliness
9. Tunnel vision
10. Minor depression
11. Loss of constructive planning
12. Plans beginning to fail
13. Idle daydreaming and wishful thinking
14. Feeling that nothing can be solved
15. Immature wish to be happy
16. Periods of confusion
17. Irritation with friends
18. Quick to anger
19. Irregular eating habits
20. Listlessness
21. Irregular sleeping habits
22. Progressive loss of daily structure
23. Periods of deep depression
24. Irregular attendance at meetings
25. Development of an "I don't care" attitude
26. Open rejection of help
27. Dissatisfaction with life
28. Feelings of powerlessness and helplessness
29. Self-pity
30. Thoughts of social gambling
31. Conscious lying
32. Complete loss of self-confidence
33. Unreasonable resentments
34. Discontinuing all treatment
35. Overwhelming loneliness, frustration, anger, and tension
36. Start of controlled gambling
37. Loss of control

What to Do When You Experience a Warning Sign

When you recognize any of these symptoms, you need to take action. Make a list of the coping skills you can use when you experience a symptom that is common for you. This will happen. You will have problems in recovery. Your task is to take affirmative action at the earliest possible moment. Remember, a symptom is a danger signal. You are in trouble. Make a list of what you are going to do. Are you going to call your sponsor, go to a meeting, call your counselor, call someone in Gamblers Anonymous, tell someone, exercise, read the *Combo Book* (Gamblers Anonymous, 1989a), pray, become involved in an activity you enjoy, turn it over, or go into treatment? Detail several plans of action.

Plan 1.

Plan 2.

Plan 3.

Plan 4.

Plan 5.

Plan 6.

Plan 7.

Plan 8.

Plan 9.

Plan 10.

You need to check each warning symptom daily in your personal inventory. You also need to have other people check you daily. You will not always pick up the symptoms in yourself. You may be denying the problem again. Your spouse, your sponsor, or a fellow GA member can warn you when he or she believes that you may be in trouble. Listen to these people. If they tell you that they sense a problem, then take action. You may need professional help in working the problem through. Do not hesitate in calling and asking for help. Anything is better than relapsing. If you overreact to a warning sign, you are not going to be in trouble. But if you underreact, you might be headed for real problems. Pathological gambling is a deadly disease. Your life is at stake.

HIGH-RISK SITUATIONS

Marlatt and Gordon (1985) found that relapse is more likely to occur in certain situations. These situations can trigger relapse. They found that people relapsed when they could not cope with life situations except by returning to their addictive behaviors. Your job in treatment is to develop coping skills for dealing with each high-risk situation.

Negative Emotions

About 35% of people who relapse do so when they feel negative feelings that they cannot cope with. Most feel angry or frustrated, but some feel anxious, bored, lonely, or depressed. Almost any negative feeling can lead to relapse if you do not learn how to cope with the emotion. Feelings motivate you to take action. You must act to solve any problem.

Circle any of the following feelings that seem to lead you to gamble.

1. Loneliness
2. Anger
3. Rejection
4. Emptiness
5. Annoyed
6. Sad
7. Exasperated
8. Betrayed
9. Cheated
10. Frustrated
11. Envious
12. Exhausted
13. Bored
14. Anxious
15. Ashamed
16. Bitter
17. Burdened
18. Foolish

19. Jealous
20. Left out
21. Selfish
22. Testy
23. Weak
24. Sorry
25. Greedy
26. Aggravated
27. Expansive
28. Miserable
29. Unloved
30. Worried
31. Scared
32. Spiteful
33. Tearful
34. Helpless
35. Neglected
36. Grief
37. Confused
38. Crushed
39. Discontented
40. Aggravated
41. Irritated
42. Overwhelmed
43. Panicked
44. Trapped
45. Unsure
46. Intimidated
47. Distraught
48. Uneasy
49. Guilty
50. Threatened

Develop a Plan to Deal With Negative Emotions

These are just a few of the feeling words. Add more if you need to do so. Develop coping skills for dealing with each feeling that makes you vulnerable to relapse. Exactly what are you going to do when you have this feeling? Detail your specific plan of action. Some options include talking to your sponsor, calling a friend in the program, going to a meeting, calling your counselor, reading some recovery material, turning it over to your Higher Power, and getting some exercise. For each feeling, develop specific plans of action.

Feeling:
Plan 1.

Plan 2.

Plan 3.

Feeling:
Plan 1.

Plan 2.

Plan 3.

Feeling:
Plan 1.

Plan 2.

Plan 3.

Continue to fill out these feeling forms until you have listed all the feelings that give you trouble and the coping skills you will use to deal with each feeling.

Social Pressure

About 20% of people relapse in social situations. Social pressure can be direct (e.g., someone directly encourages you to gamble), or it can be indirect (e.g., a social situation where people are gambling). Both of these situations can trigger intense craving, and this can lead to relapse. For example, more than 60% of alcoholics relapse in a bar.

Certain friends are more likely to encourage you to gamble. These people do not want to hurt you. They want you to relax and have a good time. They want their old friend back. They do not understand the nature of your disease. Perhaps they are pathological gamblers themselves and are in denial.

High-Risk Friends

Make a list of the friends who might encourage you to gamble.

What are you going to do when they suggest that you gamble? What are you going to say? In group, set up a situation where the whole group encourages you to gamble. How do you feel when they are encouraging you? Listen to what you say. Have them help you develop appropriate ways in which to say no.

High-Risk Social Situations

Certain social situations will trigger craving. These are the situations in which you have gambled in the past. Certain bars or restaurants, the race track, a particular part of town, certain music, athletic events, parties, weddings, and family get-togethers are some of the situations that can trigger intense cravings. Make a list of five social situations where you will be vulnerable to relapse.

1.
2.
3.
4.
5.

In early recovery, you will need to avoid these situations and friends. To put yourself in a high-risk situation is asking for trouble. If you have to attend a function where there will be gambling, then take someone with you who is in the program. Go with someone who will support you in recovery. Make sure that you have a way home. You do not have to stay and torture yourself. You can leave if you feel uncomfortable. Avoid all situations where your recovery feels shaky.

Interpersonal Conflict

About 16% of people relapse when they are in a conflict with some other person. They have a problem with someone, and they have no idea how to cope with the problem. The stress of the problem builds and leads to gambling. This conflict usually happens with someone the person is closely involved with—a spouse, child, parent, sibling, friend, or boss or another person in a similarly close relationship.

You can have a serious problem with anyone, even a stranger, so you must have a plan for dealing with interpersonal conflict. You will develop specific skills in treatment that will help you to communicate even when you are under stress.

You need to learn and repeatedly practice the following interpersonal skills.

1. Tell the truth all of the time.
2. Share how you feel.
3. Ask for what you want.
4. Find some truth in what the other person is saying.
5. Be willing to compromise.

If you can stay in the conflict and work it out, that is great. But if you cannot, you have to leave the situation and get help. You might have to go for a walk, a run, or a drive. You might need to cool down. You must stop the conflict. You cannot continue to try to deal with a situation that you believe is too much for you. Do not feel bad about this. Interpersonal relationships are the hardest challenges that we face. Carry a card with you that lists the people you can contact. You might want to call your sponsor, your minister, your counselor, a fellow Gamblers Anonymous member, a friend, a family member, your doctor, or anyone else who may support you.

In an interpersonal conflict, you will fear abandonment. You need to get accurate and reassure yourself that you have many people who still care about you. Remember that your Higher Power cares about you. God created you and loves you perfectly. Remember the other people in your life who love you. This is one of the main reasons for talking with someone else. When someone listens to you, that person gives you the feeling that you are loved.

If you still feel afraid or angry, then go to someone you trust and stay with that person until you feel safe. Do not struggle out there all by yourself. Every member of Gamblers Anonymous will understand how you are feeling. They all have had these kinds of problems. All Gamblers Anonymous members have felt lost, helpless, hopeless, and angry.

Make an emergency card that includes all of the people you can call if you are having difficulty. Write down their phone numbers and carry this card with you at all times. Show this card to your counselor or sponsor. Practice asking someone for help in treatment once each day. Write down the situation and show it to your counselor. Get into the habit of asking for help. When you get out of treatment, call someone every day just to stay in touch and keep open the lines of communication. Get used to it. Do not wait to ask for help at the last minute. This makes asking more difficult.

Positive Feelings

About 12% of people relapse when they are feeling positive emotions. Think of all the times you gambled to celebrate. That has gotten to be such a habit that when something good happens, you will immediately think about gambling. You need to be ready when you feel like a winner. This may be at a wedding, a birth, a promotion, or any event where you feel good. How are you going to celebrate without gambling? Make a celebration plan. You might have to take someone with you to a celebration, particularly in early recovery.

Positive feelings also can work when you are by yourself. A beautiful spring day can be enough to get you thinking about gambling. You need an action plan for when these thoughts pass through your mind. You must immediately get accurate and get real. In recovery, people are committed to reality. Don't sit there and imagine how wonderful you would feel if you gambled. Tell yourself the truth. Think about all of the pain that gambling has caused you. If you toy with positive gambling thoughts, you ultimately will gamble.

Circle the positive feelings that may make you vulnerable to relapse.

1. Affection
2. Bold
3. Brave
4. Calm
5. Capable
6. Boisterous
7. Confident
8. Delightful
9. Desire
10. Enchanted
11. Joy
12. Free
13. Glad
14. Glee
15. Happy
16. Honored
17. Horny
18. Infatuated
19. Inspired
20. Kinky
21. Lazy
22. Loving
23. Peaceful
24. Pleasant
25. Pleased
26. Sexy
27. Wonderful

28. Cool
29. Relaxed
30. Reverent
31. Silly
32. Vivacious
33. Adequate
34. Efficient
35. Successful
36. Accomplished
37. Hopeful
38. Orgasmic
39. Elated
40. Merry
41. Ecstatic
42. Upbeat
43. Splendid
44. Yearning
45. Bliss
46. Excited
47. Exhilarated
48. Proud
49. Aroused
50. Festive

A Plan to Cope With Positive Feelings

These are the feelings that may make you vulnerable to relapse. You must be careful when you are feeling good. Make an action plan for dealing with each positive emotion that makes you vulnerable to gambling.

Feeling:

Plan 1.

Plan 2.

Plan 3.

Feeling:
Plan 1.

Plan 2.

Plan 3.

Feeling:

Plan 1.

Plan 2.

Plan 3.

Continue this planning until you develop an approach for each of the positive feelings that make you vulnerable.

Testing Your Self-Control

About 5% of people relapse to test whether they can gamble again safely. They fool themselves into thinking that they might be able to do so normally. This time they will gamble only a little. This time they will be able to control themselves. People who fool themselves this way are in for big trouble. From the first bet, most people are in full-blown relapse within 30 days.

Testing your self-control begins with inaccurate thinking. It takes you back to Step One. You need to think accurately. You are powerless over your gambling addiction. What is true for those who are addicted to alcohol is true for you: If you use, you lose. It is as simple as that. You are physiologically, psychologically, and socially addicted to gambling. The cells in your body will not change no matter how long you are clean. You are gambling dependent in your cells. This never will change.

How to See Through Your First Temptation to Its Consequences

You need to look at how the illness part of yourself will try to convince you that you are not a problem gambler. The illness will flash on the screen of your consciousness all of the good things that gambling did for you at first. Make a list of these things. In the first column, marked "Early Gambling," write down some of the good things that you were getting out of gambling. Why were you gambling? What good came out of it? Did it make you feel social, smart, attractive, intelligent, brave, popular, desirable, relaxed, and/or sexy? Did it help you to sleep? Did it make you feel confident? Did it help you to forget your problems? Make a long list. These are the good things that you were getting when you first started gambling. This is why you were gambling.

Now go back and place in the second column, marked "Late Gambling," how you were doing in that area once you became dependent. How were you doing in that same area right before you came into treatment? Did you still feel social, or did you feel alone? Did you still feel intelligent, or did you feel stupid? You will find that a great change has taken place. The very things that you were gambling for in early gambling, you get the opposite of in late gambling. If you were gambling to be more popular, then you were feeling more isolated and alone. If you were gambling to feel brave, then you were feeling more afraid. If you were gambling to feel smart, you were feeling stupid. This is a major characteristic of pathological gambling.

Early Gambling	Late Gambling
1.	1.
2.	2.
3.	3.
4.	4.
5.	5.
6.	6.
7.	7.
8.	8.
9.	9.
10.	10.

Take a long look at both of these lists and think about how the illness is going to try to work inside of your thinking. The addicted part of yourself will present to you all of the good things that you got in early gambling. This is how the disease will encourage you to gamble. You must see through your first use of gambling to its negative consequences.

Look at the second list. You must be able to see the misery that is coming if you gamble. For most people who relapse, there are only a few days of controlled gambling before loss of control sets in. There usually are only a few hours or days before the pain begins again. Relapse is terrible. It is the most intense misery that you can imagine.

LAPSE AND RELAPSE

A lapse is the first bet. A relapse is continuing to gamble until the full biological, psychological, and social disease is present. All of the complex biological, psychological, and social components of the disease become evident very quickly.

The Lapse Plan

You must have a plan in case you lapse. It is foolish to think that you never will have a problem again. You must plan what you are going to do if you have problems. Hunt and colleagues (1971), in a study of recovering addicts, found that 33% of patients lapsed within 2 weeks of leaving treatment. Fully 60% lapsed within 3 months. At the end of 8 months, 63% had lapsed. At the end of 12 months, 67% had lapsed.

The worst thing you can do when you lapse is to think that you have completely failed in recovery. This is inaccurate thinking. You are not a total failure. You have not lost everything. You have made a mistake, and you need to learn from it. You let some part of your program go, and you are paying for it. You need to examine exactly what happened and get back into recovery.

A lapse is an emergency. It is a matter of life or death. You must take immediate action to prevent the lapse from becoming a full-blown relapse. You must call someone in the program, preferably your sponsor, and tell that person what happened. You need to carefully examine why you slipped. You cannot gamble and use the tools of recovery at the same time. Something went wrong. You did not use your new skills. You must make a plan of action to recover from your lapse. You cannot do this by yourself. You are in denial. You do not know the whole truth. If you did, then you would not have relapsed.

Call your sponsor or professional counselor and have him or her develop a new treatment plan for you. You might need to attend more meetings. You might need to see a counselor. You might need outpatient treatment. You might need inpatient treatment. You have to get honest with yourself. You need to develop a plan and follow it. You need someone else to agree to keep an eye on you for a while. Do not try to do this alone. What you cannot do alone, you can do with others.

THE BEHAVIOR CHAIN

All behavior occurs in a certain sequence. First there is the *trigger*. This is the external event that starts the behavioral sequence. After the trigger, there comes *thinking*. Much of this thinking is very fast, and you will not consciously pick it up unless you stop and focus on it. The thoughts trigger *feelings,* which give you energy and direction for action. Next comes the *behavior* or the action initiated by the trigger. Finally, there always is a *consequence* for any action.

Diagrammed, the behavior chain looks like this:
Trigger → Thinking → Feeling → Behavior → Consequence.

Let's go through a behavioral sequence and see how it works. On the way home from work, Bob, a recovering gambler, passes the convenience store (this is the trigger). He thinks, "I've had a hard day. Maybe I'll do a couple of pull tabs to unwind" (the trigger initiates thinking). Bob craves gambling (the thinking initiates feeling). He turns into the convenience store and begins to gamble (the feeling initiates behavior). Bob relapses (the behavior has a consequence).

Let's work through another example. It is 11 p.m., and Bob is not asleep (trigger). He thinks, "I'll never get to sleep tonight unless I gamble" (thinking). He feels an increase in his anxiety about not sleeping (feeling). He gets up and gambles (behavior). He loses all of his money and is so depressed that he cannot work the next morning (consequence).

How to Cope With Triggers

At every point along the behavior chain, you can work on preventing relapse. First you need to examine your triggers carefully. What environmental events lead you to gamble? We went over some of these when we examined high-risk situations. Determine what people, places, and/or things make you vulnerable to relapse. Stay away from these triggers as much as possible. If a trigger occurs, then use your new coping skills.

Do not let the trigger initiate old behavior. Stop and think. Do not let your thinking get out of control. Challenge your thinking and get accurate about what is real. Let's look at some common inaccurate thoughts.

1. It is not going to hurt.
2. No one is going to know.
3. I need to relax.
4. I am just going to spend a couple of bucks.
5. I have had a hard day.
6. My friends want me to gamble.
7. I never had a problem with sports betting.
8. It is the only way I can sleep.
9. I can do anything I want to do.
10. I am lonely.

All of these inaccurate thoughts can be used to fuel the craving that leads to relapse. You must stop and challenge your thinking until you are thinking accurately. You must replace inaccurate thoughts with accurate ones. You are a pathological gambler. If you gamble, then you will die. That is the truth. Think through the first bet. Get honest with yourself.

How to Cope With the Craving to Gamble

If you think inaccurately, then you will begin craving. This is the powerful feeling that drives compulsive gambling. Craving is like an ocean wave. It will build and then wash over you. Craving does not last long if you move away from gambling. If you move closer to a gambling situation, then the craving will increase until you gamble. Immediately on feeling a desire to gamble, think this thought:

Gambling is no longer an option for me.

Now what are your options? You are in trouble. You are craving. What are you going to do to prevent a relapse? You must move away from the gambling situation. Perhaps you need to call your sponsor, go to a meeting, turn it over, call the Gamblers Anonymous hot line, call the treatment center, call your counselor, go for a walk or run, or visit someone. You must do something besides thinking about gambling. Do not sit there and ponder gambling. You will lose that debate. This illness is called the great debater. If you leave it unchecked, then it will seduce you into gambling.

The illness must lie to work. You must uncover the lie as quickly as possible and get back to the truth. You must take the appropriate action necessary to maintain your recovery.

How to Develop a Daily Relapse Prevention Program

If you work a daily program of recovery, then your chances of success increase greatly. You need to evaluate your recovery daily and keep a log. This is your daily inventory.

1. Assess all my relapse warning signs.
   a. What symptoms did I see in myself today?
   b. What am I going to do about them?
2. Assess my love of self.
   a. What did I do to love myself today?
   b. What am I going to do tomorrow?
3. Assess my love of others.
   a. What did I do to love others today?
   b. What am I going to do tomorrow?
4. Assess my love of God.
   a. What did I do to love God today?
   b. What am I going to do tomorrow?
5. Assess my sleep pattern.
   a. How am I sleeping?
6. Assess my exercise habits.
   a. Am I getting enough exercise?
7. Assess my nutrition.
   a. Am I eating right?
8. Review my total recovery program.
   a. How am I doing in recovery?
   b. What is the next step in my recovery program?
9. Read the *Twenty-Four Hours a Day* book (Walker, 1992).
10. Make conscious contact with God.
    a. Pray and meditate for a few minutes.
    b. Relax completely.

Fill out this inventory every day following treatment and keep a journal about how you are doing. When you read back over your journal from time to time, you will be amazed at how you've changed. You will be surprised at how much you have grown.

Make a list of 10 reasons why you want to stay free from gambling.

1.
2.
3.
4.
5.
6.
7.
8.
9.
10.

Never forget these 10 reasons. Read this list and carry a copy with you. If you are struggling in recovery, then take it out and read it to yourself. You are important. No one has to live a life of misery. You can recover and live happy, joyous, and free.

Personal Recovery Plan

Name: Home Phone:
Admission Date: Work Phone:
Discharge Date: Phone:
Name of Concerned Other:

It is important to your recovery that you continue to work through your problems. Your recovery never can stand still. You must be constantly moving forward in your program. Working with your counselor or sponsor, you must detail exactly what you need to do. Each psychological problem or family problem will require a specific plan of action. You must commit yourself to following this recovery plan to the letter. Do not think that just because you have completed some parts of the program, your problems are over. Your recovery is just beginning, and you need to work diligently to stay free of your addiction to gambling.

Make a list of the problems that you need to address in continuing care. Each emotional, family, legal, social, physical, leisure, work, spiritual, or school problem will have to have a plan. How are you going to address that problem in recovery? What is the goal? What do you want to achieve? Develop your personal recovery plan with your counselor or sponsor's assistance.

Treatment Plan for Continued Abstinence From Gambling

1. Problem 1:
   Goal:
   Plan:

2. Problem 2:
   Goal:
   Plan:

3. Problem 3:
   Goal:
   Plan:

4. Problem 4:
   Goal:
   Plan:

5. Problem 5:
   Goal:
   Plan:

Relapse

In the event of a relapse, list the specific steps that you will take to deal with the problem.

Support in Recovery

Indicate the Gamblers Anonymous meetings that you will attend each week. We recommend that you attend 90 meetings in the first 90 days of recovery, then at least 1 meeting per week.

Day: Time: Location:

Indicate when you will attend any aftercare group.

Day: Time: Location:

Who is/are the Gamblers Anonymous contact person/persons who can provide you with support in early recovery?

Name: Phone:

Name: Phone:

Name: Phone:

If you have any problems or concerns during recovery, you always can call the Gamblers Anonymous National Hot Line or a center that specializes in gambling treatment.

If you and your counselor or sponsor have arranged for further counseling or treatment following discharge, then complete the following:

Name of Agency:

Address:

Phone:

First Appointment   Day: Time:

Daily Actions to Stay Free

Make a list of 10 things that you are going to do daily to stay free and away from gambling.

1.
2.
3.
4.
5.
6.
7.

    8.

    9.

    10.

High-Risk Situations to Avoid

You are changing your lifestyle. It will be important to avoid certain people and situations that will put you at high risk for returning to your previous lifestyle that supported your addiction to gambling. List the people and places you need to avoid in early recovery.

    1.

    2.

    3.

    4.

    5.

STATEMENT OF COMMITMENT

I understand that the success of my recovery depends on adherence to my recovery plan. The aftercare program has been explained to me, and I understand fully what I must do in recovery. I commit to myself that I will follow this plan.

Patient's Signature:

Signature of Counselor or Sponsor:

Date:

References

Frances, R. J., Bucky, S., & Alexopolos, G. S. (1984). Outcome study of familial and nonfamilial alcoholism. *American Journal of Psychiatry, 141,* 11.

Gamblers Anonymous (GA). (1989a). *The combo book.* Los Angeles: G.A. Publishing.

Gamblers Anonymous (GA). (1989b). *G.A.: A new beginning.* Los Angeles: G.A. Publishing.

Gorski, T. T., & Miller, M. (1982). *Counseling for relapse prevention.* Independence, MO: Independence.

Gorski, T. T., & Miller, M. (1986). *Staying sober: A guide for relapse prevention.* Independence, MO: Herald House/Independence.

Hunt, W. A., Barnett, L. W., & Branch, L. G. (1971). Relapse rates in addiction programs. *Journal of Clinical Psychology, 27,* 455-456.

Marlatt, A. G., & Gordon, J. R. (1985). *Relapse prevention.* New York: Guilford.

Perkinson, R. R. (2001). *Chemical Dependency Counseling: A Practical Guide* (2nd ed.). Thousand Oaks, CA: Sage.

Walker, R. (1992). *Twenty-four hours a day.* Center City, MN: Hazelden.

About the Author

Robert R. Perkinson, Ph.D., is the clinical director of Keystone Treatment Center in Canton, South Dakota. He has been treating alcoholics, addicts, and pathological gamblers for over 30 years. He is the author of *Chemical Dependency Counseling: A Practical Guide*, 2nd ed. (Sage, 2002), which is the leading treatment manual in the world for chemical dependency counselors. With Dr. Arthur E. Jongsma, Jr., he coauthored *The Addiction Treatment Planner*, the best-selling treatment planner and computer software program for mental health and addiction professionals. He is the author of the book *God Talks to You* and the meditation tape *A Communication From God*, which helps addicts make their first conscious contact with a higher power. He is a composer and has completed his second CD, *Peace Will Come*, which is music that helps addicts learn the essentials of a spiritual journey. Dr. Perkinson is an international motivational speaker and a regular contributor to numerous professional journals. He is the creator of several Web sites, including www.robertperkinson.com, www.alcoholismtreatment.org, www.keystonetreatment.com, and www.godtalkstoyou.com, where he answers questions on addiction and the higher power concept free of charge. His biography can be found in *Who's Who in America* and *Who's Who in the World*.